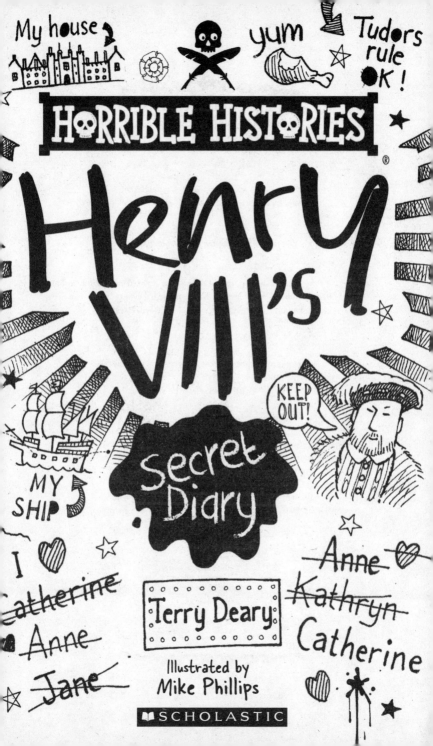

Published in the UK by Scholastic, 2021
1 London Bridge, London, SE1 9BG
Scholastic Ireland, 89E Lagan Road, Dublin Industrial Estate, Glasnevin,
Dublin, D11 HP5F

SCHOLASTIC and associated logos are trademarks
and/or registered trademarks of Scholastic Inc.

Text ©Terry Deary, 2021
Cover illustration ©Martin Brown, 2021
Text illustrations ©Mike Phillips, 2021

The right of Terry Deary, Martin Brown and Mike Phillips to be identified as the author
and illustrators of this work respectively has been asserted by them in accordance
with the Copyright, Designs and Patents Act, 1988.

ISBN 978 0702 30665 5

ACIP catalogue record for this book is available from the British Library.

Printed and bound in Great Britain by Clays Ltd, Elcograf S.p.A
Paper made from wood grown in sustainable forests and other controlled sources.

6 8 10 9 7 5

www.scholastic.co.uk

CONTENTS

That's ME!

HENRY VIII

→

I'm so
HANDSOME!

21 April 1509

Let the church bells ring. Father is DEAD.
He died of a disease of the lungs. Mother has
been dead for six years. Big brother Arthur
died the year before and that left me to
take the throne once Father popped his clogs.

Let's be honest, when Arthur died of the
sweating sickness — what some people call the
'PLAGUE' — he did us ALL a favour. He'd
have been a rotten king.

Of course, I have sisters, Margaret and Mary,
but they would have been even worse than
Arthur. And, anyway, they're girls. And girls
don't rule.

THIS IS HOW IT WORKS...

(Dad) ~~Henry VII~~ =
1457 - 1509

(Brother)
~~Arthur~~ = Catherine of
Prince of   Aragon
Wales   1485 - 1536
1486 - 1502

(Sister)
Margaret
Queen of
Scots
1489 - 1541

James IV = Margaret
of Scotland
1473 - 1513

Mary of = James V of Scotland
Guise   1512 - 1542
1515 - 1560

Francis II = Mary Stuart = Henry.
of France   Queen of Scots   Lord Darnley
1544 - 1560   1542 - 1587   1545 - 1567

James VI of Scotland
James I of England
1566 - 1625

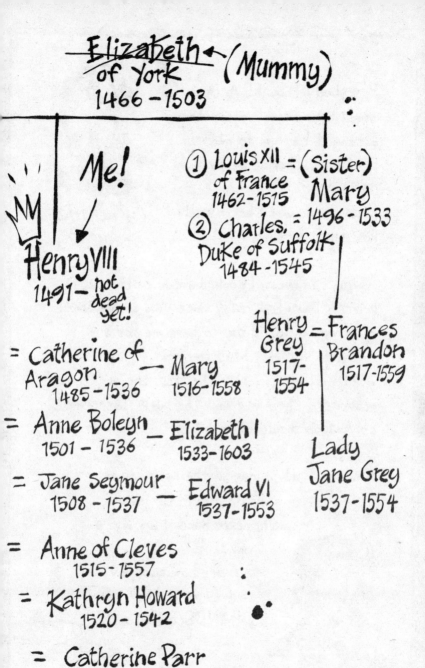

Elizabeth of York
1466 – 1503

(Mummy)

Me!

Henry VIII
1491 – not dead yet!

= Catherine of Aragon
1485 – 1536 — Mary
1516 – 1558

= Anne Boleyn
1501 – 1536 — Elizabeth I
1533 – 1603

= Jane Seymour
1508 – 1537 — Edward VI
1537 – 1553

= Anne of Cleves
1515 – 1557

= Kathryn Howard
1520 – 1542

= Catherine Parr
1512 – 1548

① Louis XII of France
1462 – 1515

= (Sister) Mary

② Charles, Duke of Suffolk
1484 – 1545

= 1496 – 1533

Henry Grey
1517 – 1554

= Frances Brandon
1517 – 1559

Lady Jane Grey
1537 – 1554

Everybody thought Arthur would have been King, so they arranged for him to marry Princess Catherine of Aragon.

I may even marry her myself, now that I'm King.

Catherine of Aragon

As you can guess, I could have any other princess I wanted really since I am so handsome ANY woman would die to have me for a husband. Not only handsome, but I play wonderful music. I play the lute, the organ, recorders, the flute and the harp. Catherine of Aragon should be so lucky.

Now it's Father playing the harp. Up in heaven. Get it? My little jest.

Oh, never mind. I am also a wonderful artist.

See how good my drawing is AND how HANDSOME I am!

Me

Henry VII is gone and a new king, Henry VIII rules. That's me, dear Diary. And let me tell you, things are going to CHANGE.

For a start, my father counted every half-penny in the palace. My mother, a queen, should have had silver buckles on her shoes. Father made her wear tin instead! His ministers say he is responsible for England's wealth. But what is the use of having riches if you don't spend it, eh? So, I shall have palaces and wars and fine clothes and GRAND FEASTS. And a navy. I think England should have a great navy.

HANDS OFF MY PIE

If the money runs out, I'll just tax the people. They should all be honoured to contribute to our great country.

Noose sense in
HANGING *around*

Then there was Father's mercy, gah!

There was a rebel called Perkin Warbeck who claimed he should be King instead of Father. He invaded TWICE. What did Father do? Granted him a position at the palace! Of course, the little traitor tried to escape, and Father had to have him hanged. Oh, dear dead Father. Why not just execute him straight away? That's what I'll be doing.

I'm not a cruel man and I won't be a cruel king. But it just makes SENSE to get rid of your enemies sharpish. Sharp as a headsman's axe.

OUCH!

I suppose I'd better get out of bed. I hate doing that. But I've got a country to rule. That lucky country is England. And a new rule starts NOW.

OR AFTER BREAKFAST ANYWAY.

17 August 1510

I have been ruling for over a year now and I must say I do enjoy it. The peasants and the servants get up with the sunrise and go to bed at sunset. In the summer that's a long time. But I am a king and I can stay in bed till as late as I like, have my breakfast served and get dressed ready for hunting.

my trusty hunting dog, KILLER!

GULP!

Oh, I know, I am supposed to be running the country but there are plenty of little ministers scuttling around like mice to do that for me. They enjoy it. It makes them feel important.

They just have to be careful that they don't begin to feel as important as I am.

And speaking of important little men who are ministers, I am going to execute a couple today. (Well, I am not going to execute them. I have a jailer in the Tower of London who does all that messy stuff for me.)

The two unlucky men are Sir Richard Empson and Edmund Dudley. They look fine in their robes, don't they? I remember them creeping around my father like two leeches sucking blood. That's Empson on the left, Father in the middle and Dudley on the right.

LOSERS!

Empson + Dudley =

Looking back to last April, I said that Father was too soft, too forgiving. What the English people need is a king who brings terror to the wicked — those who disobey. And I shall be that king.

As I also said, Father was very tight with money. And the man who collected the money was Edmund Dudley. He made just as much money for HIMSELF. You can guess the man forcing you to pay up was NOT popular. When he gets the chop people will say, 'Oh, Henry, a terrible Tudor but a good one.'

When Father was ill, Dudley raised a little army to keep the peace to prevent riots. A private army? You can't do that. It's treason. That's why he's going to the block. It doesn't matter why he did it.

As for Empson, well he is Dudley's henchman and the people despise him just as much as they do Dudley. He can go too. He'll not be money-collecting in heaven, will he?

There is a writer in Italy called Machiavelli who wrote a clever thing that I believe to be true — even more so in this instance.

> If a king has loyal people he mustn't mind if they say he is cruel from time to time. If they see him as a gentle ruler, they will plot rebellions which will lead to murders and robberies. Rebellions hurt all the people; an execution hurts no one except the person who is executed. It is better to be feared than loved.

Machiavelli

Now the people will fear me AND love me. A good day's work for the undertaker.

30 April 1513

My father defeated Richard III in battle back in 1485. The evil Richard had said that if anything happened to him in the battle, then Edmund de la Pole was to have his crown. Of course, when Richard III was killed, Father was worried that friends of Richard would invite de la Pole to lead a rebellion.

Before Father died, he wrote a will, and in that will he told me to execute de la Pole. In my kindness, I decided to keep him locked in the Tower of London instead. One of our finest palaces. Maybe I did inherit some of Father's 'mercy' after all.

Tower of London

The Tower of London

drawn by Me... The King!

Barrack

St. Peter's Chapel

The Moat

Legge's Mount

Scaffold (for head removal)

Bell Tower

King's House

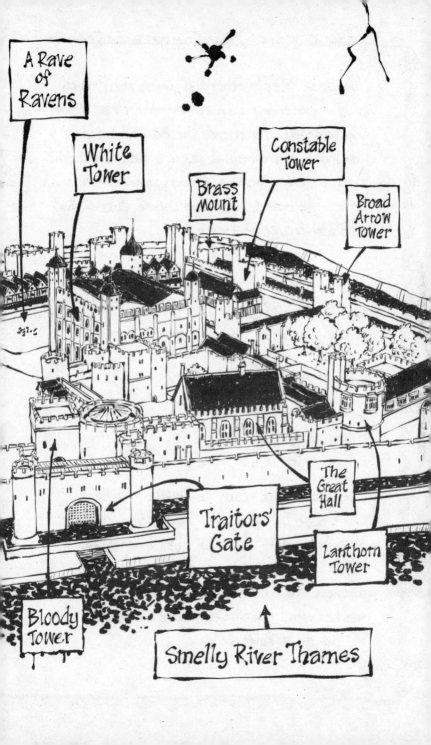

Now de la Pole's brother has joined the French army – our enemy. I am at war with France, for goodness sake. My friend, the Admiral Lord Howard, was drowned at sea in a battle with the French. He was wearing armour, so once he was forced overboard, he had no chance. A brick had a better chance of floating.

OOPS!!!

well, he made a splash

I am just about ready to invade France. I can't have Edward de la Pole – the brother of a traitor – sitting in the Tower, waiting to be saved by his brother like a damsel in distress. No, the execution is what my father wanted. And I shall sleep more easily with one of the de la Poles dead.

Usually I stick the heads of the executed traitors on a spike over London Bridge to show the people what happens to those who plot against me. Maybe I should do that with Ed's dead head? It would give my loyal London subjects plenty of amusement. I can picture them now.

Now, I need to plan my invasion of France. Of course, I'll need money to pay my army to thrash the Frenchies, so I will just tax the people. After all, I am fighting the French to save the English people from being invaded. If that happens, they'll all end up speaking French, and they won't like that.

Giovanni Medici is the new pope, Leo X, and he's promised to attack France from Italy in the south while I sail across the Channel and attack the Frenchies from the north. I'll have to move fast and raise money even faster.

My best man for the MONEY-GRABBING job is Thomas Wolsey. I like his style.

I'll get him to do the taxing. He's a clever chap. I think I'll soon be making him my top minister — my chancellor. And that shows what a clever king I am.

You understand that, don't you, dear Diary? If I told the people to give me money for the wars, they would hate me — hate me the way they hated Sir Richard Empson and Edmund Dudley.

'A rich king taxing the poor people,'

they would cry and snivel and drivel.

But Thomas Wolsey is one of them. The lowly. A man of the people. His father was a butcher from Ipswich, and you can't get more lowly than that, can you?

Cunning Thomas doesn't mind doing the unpopular jobs and the boring jobs. I will make him the greatest common man in England.

20 June 1514

Scotland. SCOTLAND.

A torment I have to suffer. You remember, dear Diary, that last year I fought in France. As soon as I sailed across the English Channel, the treacherous Scots invaded the north of England. That villainous Scots King James IV – married to my SISTER – attacked our backs while I was fighting bravely in France (for my dear friend, the Pope).

My wife Catherine chose the Earl of Surrey to defend our noble land. Surrey? He was 70 years old. But the old man did a good job. He marched north – at least, Surrey was CARRIED north. And met the Scots as they crossed the border at a place called Flodden.

26

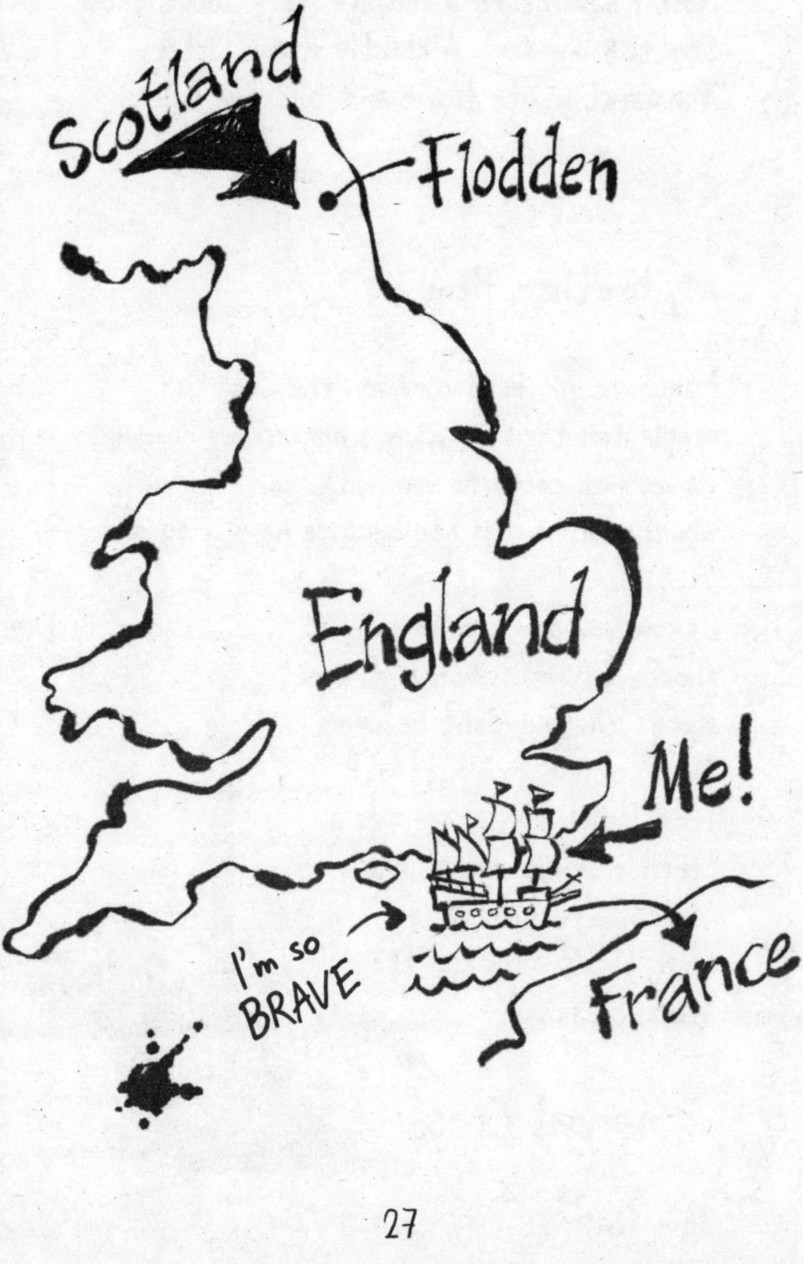
Scotland
Flodden
England
Me!
I'm so
BRAVE
France

Now, I have heard a strange story about those Scottish invaders. A ghostly story. Sister Margaret wrote to me and told the tale...

My brother, Henry,

I am sure you have forgiven the Scottish people for their invasion. I begged my husband James not to go to war with you. I knew it would cost him his life because he was cursed.

I know you don't believe in ghosts, but it is such a strange story. On the night before the Scottish Army set off from Edinburgh there was a terrible cry heard at the Mercat Cross. (That's what the English call the Market Cross.)

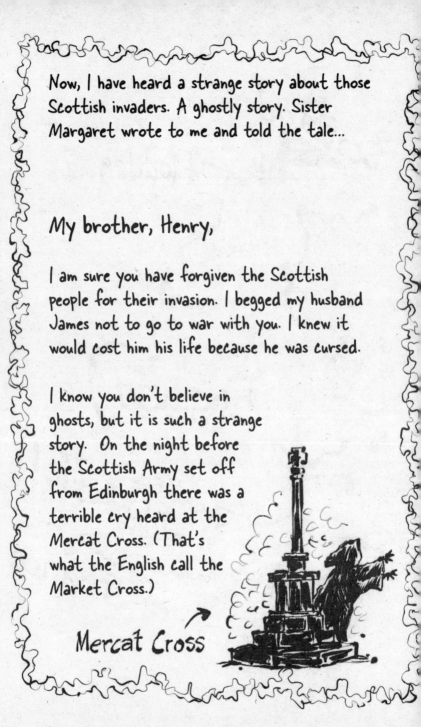

Mercat Cross

The horrifying howl called out, 'The following men are doomed to die ... First, King James...'

The voice wailed out the names of the lords and knights who would die in the war. No one knew if the voice was a human's or a spirit's ... but the men marched off to fight at Flodden. And the men who were named never came back alive.

A man called Richard Lawson said he saw the cursing crier and it was the Devil himself. Some people think this REALLY happened ... but it wasn't a ghost and it wasn't the Devil. It was all a trick by me, Queen Margaret, to stop my husband going off to war. James was killed anyway at the battle of Flodden Field. It was not me. How would I know those men would die?

Your loving and loyal sister,

Margaret

My wife, Catherine, was given King James's blood-soaked coat and she sent it to me in France. She thought I could use it as a banner in the battle. She even said she'll send the dead king's body. I was angry that she was boasting about 'her' victory. She'll not do that again.

I decided the best way to keep the Scots out was for me to cause trouble on the border between us. I've been sending my men from Northern England to raid the Scottish border towns and keep the Scots too busy to make war. My stout fellows have plundered, burned and killed with great cruelty. They left famine and destruction behind them. Towns and houses were burned. Cattle and sheep were taken by the hundreds and crops destroyed. Stick that in your bagpipes, you Scottish savages.

And NOW I receive a report that the tormented Scots have fought back!

HOW DARE THEY?

Sire,

The men of Hawick Town were mostly killed at Flodden. But last night a gathering of their sons collected old spears, pikes, clubs and rusting swords, bows and arrows and attacked our army as we slept in our tents at a place called Hornshole. They rode horses and drove cattle over the tents and crushed us terribly. I am sure Your Highness will want to send more men to avenge this cowardly Scottish massacre.

Your humble servant,

Thomas Howard, Earl of Surrey

Scots? A plague, a curse and a thorn in my side.

I SHALL BE AVENGED.

25 December 1517

It is Christmas and how I love this time of the year. The poor shiver in their winter hovels. They'll kill the family pig and make it last all winter for their watery dinners. But I am a king and I shall live — and eat — like one.

I shall have log fires burning in my halls and have all the fun a king deserves. Last night we had dancers and jugglers, acrobats and singers, jesters and a dancing bear. (The bear had to be whipped to make it move and the blood splashed on the dress of one of my queen's maids. I noticed how pretty she was so I helped her wipe off the blood.)

Everyone cried out that none of the singers were as good as me. The lords and ladies at our feast even begged me to take out my lute and sing for them. Of course, I did. I sang a song I wrote especially for Christmas. But it

was also a love song. And the young maid of
my queen had caught my eye. I am sure her
heart leapt when I looked at her as I sang...

My Lute

Farewell, my own lady,
Farewell, my special,
Who has my heart truly,
Be sure, she ever shall.

Green grows the holly, so does the ivy.
Though winter blasts blow ever so high,
Green grows the holly.

Oh, how my guests clapped and cheered. I had
to sing it again. And again. If I were not busy
being King, then I should be England's greatest
musician. I found out the maid's name is
Anne Boleyn.

Then there was the feasting. The cook
showed me what we'd be eating...

First course:

Grilled Beaver's Tails.
Whale Meat.
Wild Boar Meat.
Roast Tongue.
Leg of Pork.
Roast Beef.
Roast Deer.
Meat Pie and Vegetables,
with bread and wine.

Second course:

Whole Roasted Peacock.
Roast Lamb.
Swan.
Rabbit.
Bread.
Sugared Fruit.
Gingerbread.
Sugared Almonds.
Spiced Fruitcake.

I will have spent £8,000 on feasts for the twelve days of Christmas. My miserable father didn't even spend £12,000 for TWELVE MONTHS in his palaces. I will show our guests from France and Spain just how rich England is.

And in the centre of the dinner table is the boar's head from the wild boar I killed myself on this morning.

Of course, I also hunted deer and we ate the flesh in a pie. As a special Christmas treat, we gave the servants the inside of the animal to eat. We call these the umbles and they bake it into umble pie. My cook showed me the recipe he uses.

WHAT AN OFFAL MESS!

Umble pie

Ingredients:

Deer umbles — the heart, liver, tongue, feet, ears and brains chopped up and mixed with beef, oysters, bacon and rabbit. Dried fruit and pastry

To cook:

Stew the umbles and the other meat till tender then place in a pie dish. Cover the stewed umbles with the dried fruit and a crust.

Bake till the crust is crisp and brown.

I made this on the hoof!

Then my favourites. The actors who perform their MUMMERS Play. I have seen it every year since I was a child. First comes the man in green – Father Christmas – and I know his words better than any actor. I could easily play that part.

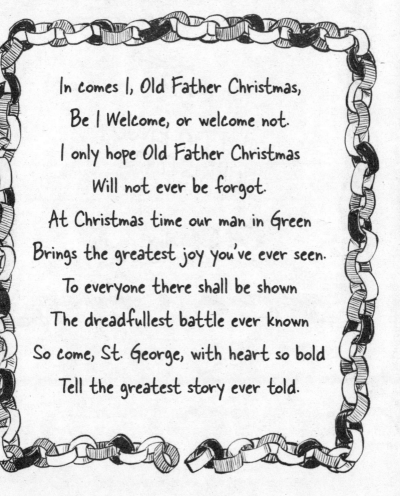

In comes I, Old Father Christmas,

Be I Welcome, or welcome not.

I only hope Old Father Christmas

Will not ever be forgot.

At Christmas time our man in Green

Brings the greatest joy you've ever seen.

To everyone there shall be shown

The dreadfullest battle ever known

So come, St. George, with heart so bold

Tell the greatest story ever told.

Then in comes Saint George — a hero in armour, just like me in real life. There are sword fights and at last Saint George sets the captive princess free.

OH, I DO ENJOY CHRISTMAS.

3 September 1518

The plague is back in England. How my poor people are suffering. And then there is also the 'sweating sickness', which is killing even more people.

Death has strolled through the land with his scythe, mowing down some and missing others.

People say they have seen him taking lives with a swish of that scythe.

Ooooooh, SCARY! →

As an Italian doctor wrote...

> *There appeared certain swellings in the groin and under the armpit, the victims spat blood, and in three days they were dead.*

My own doctors have told me these swellings would ooze with blood and pus. Purple-black blotches appeared on the skin and you would smell absolutely revolting. Swell, spit, smell, swish. You are gone.

But I wouldn't know. I haven't seen Death and I haven't seen anyone with the plague.

In the streets of London, they say the piles of bodies grow like chopped straw into a haystack. They are loaded onto carts, then dropped into pits – in France, they throw the bodies in the river.

Our daughter Mary is a worry. She is just two years old and children are Death's particular favourites when it came to the swish.

A preacher has said the children probably got what they deserved. He explained...

"It may be that children suffer heaven's revenge because they miss going to church or because they hate their fathers and mothers. God kills children with the plague — as you can see every day — because, according to the old law, children who are rebels (or disobedient to their parents) are punished by death."

God sent the plague; the doctors must cure it. My doctor has told me I could catch it by looking at a victim, by breathing bad air or by

41

drinking from poisoned wells. I shall do none of these things. I believe some cures are as bad as the sickness. A medical book has said...

A PERSON WITH THE PLAGUE SHOULD TRY THESE CURES...

- sit in a sewer so the bad air of the plague is driven off by the worse air of the drains

- drink a medicine of ten-year-old treacle

- swallow powders of crushed emeralds

- eat arsenic powder

- try letting blood out of the patient (when your horoscope is right)

- kill all the cats and dogs in the town

- shave a live chicken's bottom and strap it to the plague sore

- march from town to town flogging yourself with a whip

The doctors check the urine of their patients. If there is blood in it then there is no hope.

But I can tell you, dear Diary, that the only 'cure' that works is to escape the rat-infested towns to the countryside. The rich people, with country houses like myself, can do this. The poor stay at home and die.

I feel sorry for them, of course, but I shall pray for them.

I do not want you to think I am a coward. I am NOT a coward and I am not running away. I could stay in London and catch plague. A man as strong as I am could defeat it. (I have a box of emeralds that I can crush and eat.)

But I have to save the life of poor baby Mary. Mary is the only reason I am leaving London for a year. I am such a good father.

25 June 1520

France. FRANCE.

An even greater plague than Scotland OR the sweating sickness.

I went to war with them back in 1513, captured a couple of their cities and forced them to make peace in 1514. Wolsey drew up a fine peace treaty with French king, Louis XII. Good chap, Wolsey. He even came up with a plan to ban all wars in Europe. That's never going to happen. Too many French and Spanish LIKE fighting.

And everyone LOVES to see me in my armour. ➡

Me →

To make sure we stayed at peace, Wolsey had the idea of marrying off my sister Mary to King Louis. Mary is a pretty girl, I guess.

Mary Queen of France →

And we've always been close. Why, I even named my daughter after her. But my sister was not very pleased at being married off to Louis. 'I'm 18 and he's 52!' she argued.

Still, she knew it was her duty.

'I'll tell you what,' I said. 'When Louis dies, then I'll let you marry anyone you want next time around. Agreed?' She agreed.

But I didn't expect Louis would do what he did next, did I? After two months he only went and died, didn't he? I was annoyed, I can tell you.

But not half as annoyed as I was when Mary ran off and married her old love, Charles Brandon. As you know, dear Diary, you can NOT marry a royal princess unless the King (me) agrees. It is treason. I wanted Brandon's head on a spike (even though he is my best friend). But I love my little sister and Wolsey talked me out of it. So I let Brandon keep his head and made him pay a huge fine instead.

King Francis I

Anyway, Louis' son – the new king of France – is Francis I. He's a nasty piece of work, but he took the throne and I had to make a new peace agreement with him.

He invited me over to France. He said we could talk about peace and have a great tournament while I was there. I love a good tournament, so I agreed. I've just returned from there now.

Of course, foul French Francis wanted to outshine me with dazzling tents, fancy clothes, huge feasts, music, jousting and games. Red wine even flowed from two fountains and his tents were made with so much cloth of gold that the meeting place was named after it. THE FIELD OF THE CLOTH OF GOLD.

BLING, BLING!

But the tallest tent of all was blown down in a gale and that gave me a laugh. Served Francis right. What a show-off.

We agreed that we two kings would not compete against each other. In the mock battles we fought on the same side. In one of the battles, Francis was smashed in the face and got a bloody nose. My poor, dear, French brother. I had to laugh.

Towards the end of the meeting, we watched French wrestlers, (including two priests), fighting against the English in wrestling matches. It was so exciting I grabbed Francis by the collar and challenged him to a match. I expected to win.

Grrrrr!

I WAS ROBBED!

But that crooked French king used a filthy French trip to put me on the floor. And then — THEN he had to tell people he'd won. I did NOT lose, I was CHEATED.

In revenge I showed off my archery skills and challenged Francis to shoot my own longbow. Hah, he wasn't even strong enough to draw back the string. I had to laugh. A win to me, I think.

And for all his showy tents, we English came up with the greatest sight of all. The crowds all looked on in wonder as a dragon flew through the sky. Of course, my 'dragon' was a kite made by my workmen from canvas stretched around wooden hoops. It was pulled across the sky at the end of a long rope tied to a carriage. The dragon's eyes blazed, and its mouth hissed as I'd had it filled with fireworks. Young Miss Boleyn said it was wonderful. Sweet girl.

what a
DRAG-ON

I have to say that some people were miserable. They moaned about the food we wasted while English peasants starved in the fields and ditches. John Fisher, Bishop of Rochester, wrote...

> *Where be all those pleasures now? They were but shadows, and like shadows they be past, like shadows they be fled away, like shadows they be now vanished from us.*

Party pooper. All in all, it was a GOOD meeting and the English came out better. Or should I say I,

King Henry, came out better?

11 October 1521

A great end to the year after a bad start. In April, I had to execute the Duke of Buckingham because he was plotting to kill me. He never admitted it, but his servants betrayed him. At first, his lying servants said they knew nothing, but after a few hours in the Tower of London torture chambers they started to spill words like a waterfall. My torturers are VERY good. I like the rack myself...

He was in for a LONG stretch

The Rack ↲

As the year went on there was more trouble with the new menace in Europe. Our church, led by our dear Pope, is under attack from a group of people called Protestants ... because they 'protest' against the Catholic Church.

They are led by a man called Martin Luther in Germany. I have just read a leaflet full of the dreadful lies these Protestants are spreading.

On 31 October 1517 Martin Luther nailed a bit of paper to a church door. Millions have died since that simple but Awful Act.

The trouble is that most people in Europe believe what the church tells them. Priests say, 'Give us your cash and we will have a word with God. He'll make sure you go to heaven. So, pay up.'

The payments are called 'indulgences'. People paid. Then the Pope decided to build an even bigger palace for himself in Rome. He needed money, so he ordered his priests, 'Charge more for the indulgences.'

The German monk, Martin Luther, was angry. He said the Pope was rich enough ... and, anyway, indulgences were a daft idea. God would let people into heaven without them. Luther wrote his ideas on this paper and nailed them to the church door at All Saints Church in Wittenberg.

Lots of people agreed with Luther and made their own church – the Protestant Church. And THAT made endless trouble ... since Luther's time millions of Protestants have been horribly slaughtered by Catholics – millions of Catholics have been horribly slaughtered by Protestants.

Some of the world's most horrible history has been Catholic Christians hating Protestant Christians. They have:

- roasted children over an open fire and peeled off the skin of living men

- chopped off hands and feet and thrown them over town walls

- thrown women down wells and piled stones on top of them

- pulled out the eyes of soldiers and sliced off their noses and lips

- tortured priests by stretching them on racks till their bones cracked

- nipped off lumps of flesh with red-hot pincers

- … hanged men in their own gardens while their wives and children watched

- beheaded an old lady with 20 axe blows

- hanged people in chains and left them to die slowly

Martin Luther nailed his list to the church door at Wittenberg.

Lies and nonsense. I wrote a book called <u>The Defence of the Seven Sacraments</u>; a fine book that explained why Luther is a liar and a lout.

The trusty Wolsey and my old friend, the Bishop of Rochester, have made a pile of these leaflets and books and BURNED them. (Not MY book, oh no.) Of course, Wolsey wants to be the next Pope so this sort of action will help him. A butcher's son as Pope? Stranger things have happened.

And on this day, dear Diary, the Pope Leo X has given me yet another title: 'Defender of the Faith', for writing my book.

God must be smiling down on me this day. He's probably reading my book right now.

22 October 1526

Dear Diary, I have a problem. My wife, Catherine of Aragon, was engaged to be married to my brother, Arthur, as you know. It would keep the peace between England and Spain. Arthur died. I didn't mind that so much because it meant I became King. And Father said I should marry Catherine in his place, so the deal with Spain could go ahead.

Catherine of Aragon

Catherine is six years older than I am and a pleasant enough woman. The trouble is England needs a strong king after I've gone. That may be around 60 years from now — or even longer; after all, I am incredibly strong — but it is my duty to make sure I have a son and heir to the throne.

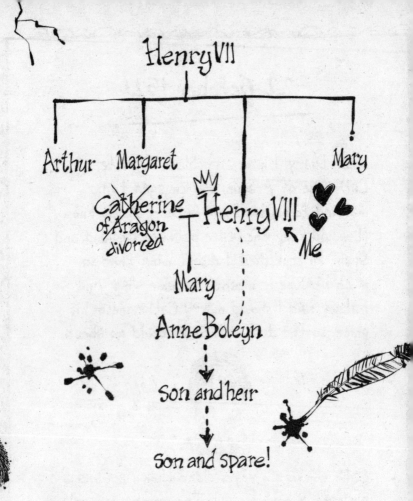

Henry VII

- Arthur
- Margaret
- ~~Catherine of Aragon~~ divorced — Henry VIII ♥♥♥ ← Me
  - Mary
- Mary

Anne Boleyn
↓
Son and heir
↓
Son and spare!

All Catherine has given me is a daughter, Mary, and a lot of dead babies. And now she is getting too old to have any more. Sorry, Catherine, but the only answer is for me to divorce you and marry someone younger. Maybe someone like Anne Boleyn.

In February I was jousting — and I did jolly well. Anne was on the throne in the gallery. I think everyone knows where this is heading.

There's one problem. Because I am a king, I need to get the Pope to agree to my divorce. It's all right for common people to divorce. But because I am special, I have this special rule. The other problem is my old friend, Pope Leo X, died three years ago. He was the one who made me 'Defender of the Faith' so he would have immediately said, 'Yes' to a silly little thing like a divorce.

Now, we have Clement VII as Pope and he is a miserable old trout...

Spot the difference

But not to fret, dear Diary. I came up with a plan to make him see what a good Christian I am. You see, there's this chap called Tyndale who wrote the Bible in ENGLISH instead of Latin. Tyndale says the peasants will understand it ... if the priests read it to them in church. (The peasants can't read, of course, oh dear me, no.) But we can't have them listening to the Bible in English. So, on 6 February, I got my good old Bishop John Fisher to make a pile of all of Tyndale's Bibles. He made a bonfire of them in London. Splendid fellow, Fisher.

And on a frosty London day the crowds must have been pleased by the warmth.

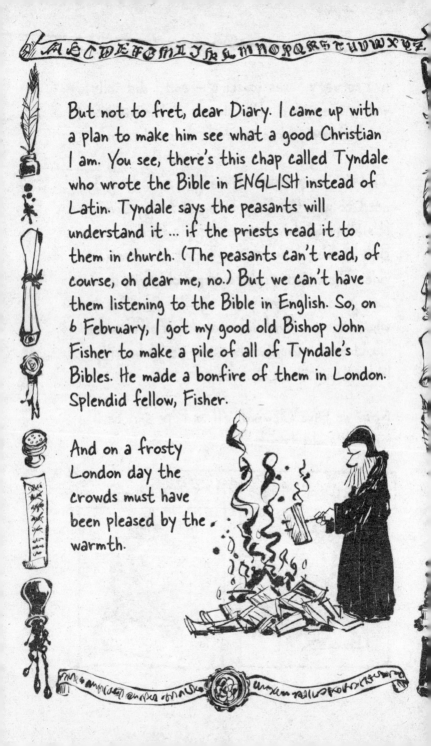

If THAT is not enough to please miserable old Pope Clement VII, then today I have had a report from Cuthbert Tunstall.

22 October 1526

Your Highness,

I am sending you a report which PROVES that the dreadful Tyndale Bible has more than 2,000 mistakes. If it is used in churches, then the English people will be led into the paths of The Devil.

Your most humble Lord Keeper of the Seal

Cuthbert Tunstall.

I shall send a copy to Pope Clement to show what a good defender of the faith I am. If that does not work, then I shall send my dearest minister Wolsey to get me my divorce.

It WILL happen and Anne SHALL be my wife.

23 June 1527

It is done, dear Diary. Yesterday I told Catherine that I wanted to divorce her. I think she guessed but there were still floods of tears. I can't stand the sight of women crying. I told her I had to go out hunting and rode down here to Bolebroke Castle near Ashdown Forest.

Bolebroke Castle

It lies only 5 miles from Hever Castle — the home of the Boleyn family. Maybe it won't be the only deer I am hunting. (Deer ... dear? See? Oh, I am such a wit.)

The sweating sickness is in London, so it was sensible of me to move to one of my country palaces like Bolebroke. I can still rule from here, but it means I can also go hunting every day. I have made hunting parks in London, but they are too small to give me a full morning's hunting. This sweating sickness may kill a few hundred common people, but I rather enjoy my trips to my hunting lodge to hunt for deer.

Today we were up at first light, around 5 o'clock in the morning and, on this adventure, we planned to hunt stags. There are wild boars near here, but they are too slow to be much fun to hunt and slaughter. Deer — and stags — are far trickier. I ride after them and use my javelin to kill them. Not many hunters can throw a javelin from a moving horse and bring down a fleeing deer as it dodges through the trees, squealing with fear.

Some hunters use guns — I have one myself...

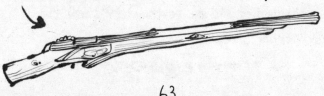

But guns will NEVER be as popular as bows and spears.

Anne carried a bow and arrow. All she hit was a cow. A COW. Oh, I laughed so much I almost fell from my saddle.

Oooops

BULLSEYE!

Now farmers can hunt foxes to save their chickens. And peasants hunt hedgehogs because they are said to suck the milk from their cows. A peasant can claim four pence for every hedgehog they kill. Kingfishers steal our fish, ravens steal our grain, woodpeckers destroy our forests. All wild animals have to be killed and my hunting is not cruel. I am just helping my people get rid of pests. Deer chew the bark from trees.

And, of course, they are good to eat.

I chased one for an hour till it was exhausted and turned to face me. I waited till cow-killer Anne caught up with me, raised my javelin, took aim and threw it.

I hit the stag between the antlers, and it fell.

LOOK AT ME!

No thanks

Anne clapped her tiny white hands and cried out in joy. The servants dragged the animal back to Bolebroke and tonight we feasted well after a game of bowls on the lawn. Anne was my partner in the game. Her skill with the bowl is better than her skill with the bow. A good jest, I think... Well, Anne laughed. We won.

After the feast, I asked Miss Boleyn to stay the night at Bolebroke, but she said it was her duty to stay with her parents. She will stay with me when she is my wife.

29 November 1530

Wolsey has failed me. He is a fool. NO ONE
FAILS HENRY VIII.

All he had to do was get me a divorce from
Catherine. But the Pope is still refusing. What
a disaster that idiot Wolsey is.

Wolsey was up in York and I sent an order that
he was to be arrested. He was commanded to
come to London to stand trial. Anne wants his
head on a spike. She never liked him.

'What can I charge him with, my sweet?'
I asked her.

'You'll think of something,' she told me.
'You are so clever.'

Of course, Anne is right. I am probably the
smartest man in England. But Wolsey cheated

me at the end. As he travelled to London he stopped at Leicester and there he died. I will not see his head on the arch over London Bridge where it belongs.

Why don't I bring his head back, you are asking, dear Diary? You see, the June before last, one of Anne's ladies died from the sweating sickness. I saved myself by going to another palace 12 miles away and ordered Anne to go home to her parents at Hever Castle in Kent. A charming place that I've visited in secret a few times...

Anne DID have the sickness, so I was wise to send her away. She lived because I had prayers said for her in every church and God listens to me.

If Wolsey died of the sickness, I do NOT want his body brought to London. Let his evil body rot. He made far too much money from the people of England. He made so much money he built one of the finest palaces in the country: Hampton Court.

A quick pic of Me outside.
Hampton Court Palace

←Me

Hampton Court is mine now and I shall move from old Westminster Palace with my dearest Anne.

Of course, I have a much better 'Thomas' to take Wolsey's place. Thomas More is a wise and powerful man. Together we shall make England the greatest country in the world.

AND I SHALL HAVE MY DIVORCE.

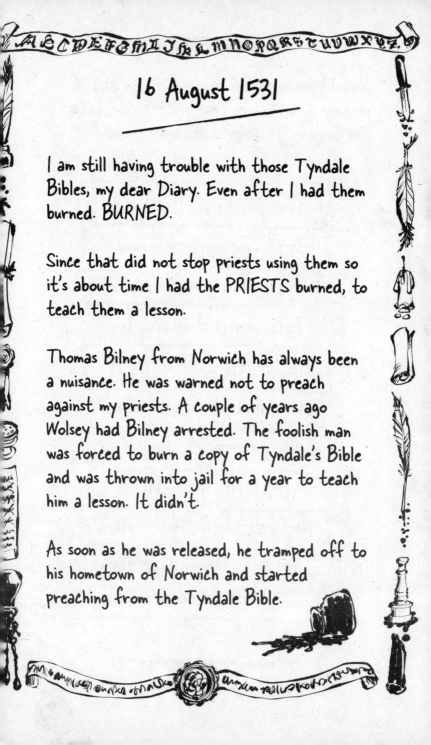

16 August 1531

I am still having trouble with those Tyndale Bibles, my dear Diary. Even after I had them burned. BURNED.

Since that did not stop priests using them so it's about time I had the PRIESTS burned, to teach them a lesson.

Thomas Bilney from Norwich has always been a nuisance. He was warned not to preach against my priests. A couple of years ago Wolsey had Bilney arrested. The foolish man was forced to burn a copy of Tyndale's Bible and was thrown into jail for a year to teach him a lesson. It didn't.

As soon as he was released, he tramped off to his hometown of Norwich and started preaching from the Tyndale Bible.

Now I have read this Bible and it is full of strange new phrases that will NEVER enter the English language. Just look at them!

'the powers that be'

'my brother's keeper'

'the salt of the earth'

'a law unto themselves'

'fight the good fight'

'twinkling of an eye'

'let there be light'

'gave up the ghost'

'the signs of the times'

'the spirit is willing, but the flesh is weak'

Well, this power that be is a law unto himself and says let there be light … the light of a fire under Bilney's foolish feet. And once the fire is lit, he will give up the ghost because his spirit may be willing, but his flesh is weak.

(I think that what I did with his words is rather clever, don't you?)

A report from my law officer in Norwich told what happened next…

Bilney approached the stake in a plain gown, his arms hanging out, his hair mangled by the monks tearing off his priest's robes. Bilney was allowed to speak to the crowd and told them not to blame the monks for his death. He said his private prayers.

The sheriff's men then put the reeds and logs about his body, and set fire to the reeds, which made a great blaze, and blackened his face; but the flames were blown away from him several times, the wind being very high, till at length the logs took fire, the flame was stronger. He cried out 'Jesus' and 'I believe', and so he yielded up the ghost.

I wish I had seen that, but I was travelling the country to meet my people. As Bilney cooked, I was watching a pleasant game of 'football'. The mayor of the town explained the rules.

Two teams of about 150 on each side from two rival villages. They meet in a large meadow around a quarter-of-a-mile long.

A goal is marked at each end of the meadow. The lord of the manor throws the ball from the walls of the castle and it is carried to the field. It is a pig's bladder blown till it is hard.

The ball is placed in the middle. Both teams rush for the ball and try to score a goal by kicking the ball over the other team's goal line.

The first team to score TWO goals is the winner. At the end the ball is thrown into the river and a player from each side swims after it. The player who gets the ball and carries it across to the other side gets to keep the ball.

There are no other rules, but there must be no guns, knives or spears.

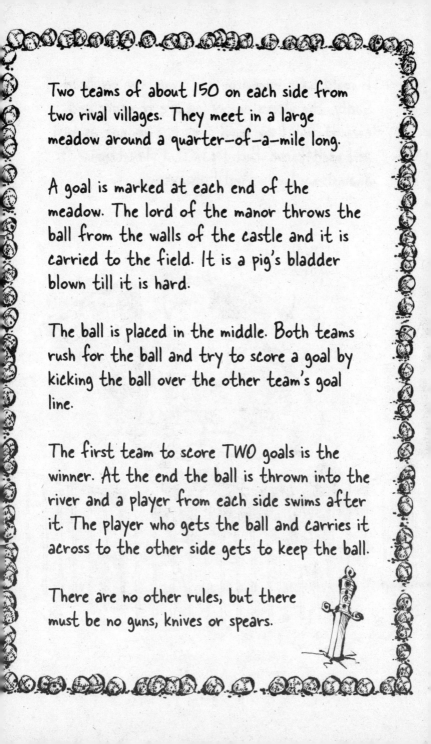

I would have joined in AND won for my team. Sadly, the ulcers on my leg are too sore and even though I am VERY fast, I am not as fast as I used to be. But I can still play tennis against my lords. And I always win.

LOVE ME!

14 November 1532

Anne and I are married. It was all done in secret. It has to be at the moment.

We cannot continue to wait for the foolish Pope to give me my divorce.

We had a fine wedding feast, but I was careful what I ate. You remember the case of Richard Roose that I told you about in May?

He was the cook to my dear friend, John Fisher, the Bishop of Rochester. You remember? The bishop who burned Tyndale Bibles for me.

Last year, he held a grand dinner and his cook, Richard Roose, sprinkled a white powder in some of the pottage. The powder would make them run to the toilets all night long. It seems Roose thought it would be a good joke.

In fact, seventeen of the bishop's guests were very ill and two died. Now, as you know, I am scared of nothing and no man. But I hate the idea of poison. I am sure that one day someone will try to poison me. After all, there isn't a single man who wouldn't kill to be me.

So, I went to Roose's trial in the House of Lords. The lords said he had to hang. I argued:

For a crime like that he should be boiled alive in his own cooking pot.

Sorry, Your Highness, but the law does not allow us to boil people alive.

Then CHANGE the law.

And that's what they did. From then on, poisoners were to be boiled alive and that was how Roose died. He was taken to Smithfield on 5 April 1531 and boiled to death. It is said that people who watched the execution were so shocked that they were carried away as if 'half-dead'. Good. That'll teach them to think twice before trying to poison ME.

Fisher is not very fond of my lovely Anne or the Boleyn family. There are rumours that the Boleyns ordered Roose to poison old Fisher, their enemy. All nonsense, of course. My lovely Anne and her family are the best people on this island.

But Fisher needs to be careful. When he attacks the Boleyns, he attacks me. And attacking Henry VIII, as you know dear Diary, is never wise.

7 September 1533

A bad day for poor Henry, dear Diary. And a bad day for England. It seems this king is cursed.

Anne married me on 25 January, in private.

Anne was crowned Queen of England on 1 June 1533 but Thomas More refused to come to the coronation. He had better be careful.

The coronation was a fine event that lasted four days. Anne sailed down the Thames. Flags hung with gold foil that glittered in the sun and rang with little bells.

row, row, row your boat gently down the...

The barges were packed with musicians of every kind and the fleet was led by a boat that held a mechanical dragon. It could be made to move and belch out flames. There were other models of monsters and huge wild men, who threw blazing fireworks and uttered blood-chilling screams.

The streets were decorated with banners that had our names twined together H for Henry and A for Anne. 'HA'.

As we passed by, the London crowds pointed at the banners and cried, 'HA! HA! HA!'. Some of my lords thought the people were mocking us. But I know they love me. They wouldn't do anything of the sort. It is true they are not fond of Anne, but they would never dare make fun of us.

The greatest event of all should have been today when Anne gave birth to our son, my heir. Instead she gave birth to a daughter. I am furious. Of course, I shall name the child Elizabeth after my mother. I shall love it. But Anne must give me a son.

And I must get that divorce from Pope Clement. Thomas More is no better than Thomas Wolsey was. And we know what happened to Wolsey, don't we, dear Diary?

The matter has been put in the hands of yet another Thomas — Thomas Cromwell.

Cromwell will also take care of the case against Elizabeth Barton, the so-called Holy Maid of Kent. She has been telling people that if I married Anne, I'd be dead in a few months. I am still here. It is Elizabeth Barton who will die. I shall have her hanged.

Foolish woman. Telling the King he will die is a crime.

30 March 1534

That's done it. Today a new law was passed.
It says my marriage to Catherine was not legal
because she was engaged to my brother,
Arthur. Catherine and I were never married.
Thomas Cromwell – a terrific chap – has
done what Thomas Wolsey and Thomas More
failed miserably to do.

Cromwell is a common man just like Wolsey
was. Cromwell's father was a blacksmith.
Cromwell once told my Archbishop Cranmer...

> I used to be a bit of a ruffian
> in my young days.

Well, I like ruffians. They get things done.

The Pope has been refusing me a divorce for
six years.

You could say I gave myself a divorce today. I sent out a message to my people...

I am, God be thanked, King of England, and in times past the Kings of England never had any lord but God.

MINE

Henry VIII

Pope Clement will be so angry when he reads that. Except I hear he is a sick man. Some people are saying he was fed poisoned mushrooms. Who knows? So long as he dies soon, I shall be happy.

I am not a man who doesn't care about death. Last year, my sister Mary died. She caught the sweating sickness back in 1528 and has never been well since. Mary was my sister and my friend. I do miss her.

And to add to my misery, there is a rebellion in Ireland. This time the rebel is my cousin – Thomas Fitzgerald. I called Tom's father to London and some rumour went back to Cousin Tom. It said I'd executed his father. Nonsense. I wouldn't execute one of my own family, would I?

His soldiers wear silk fringes on their helmets.

So, they call him Silken Thomas.

Tom rode into Dublin at the head of his little army and threw down a sword in St Mary's Abbey. That sword is the sign that Tom rules Ireland for me. The message is clear ... Silken Thomas rules Ireland.

My archbishop in Dublin tried to flee to England for safety but his ship was wrecked on the Irish coast, and he fell into the hands of Silken Tom. What did the Silken savage do? I have a report here...

Silken Thomas handed the archbishop over to his soldiers, who brained and hacked him in gobbets.

I have enough problems. Why does Cousin Thomas make things worse? It isn't fair on poor me.

22 June 1535

Today, dear Diary, Bishop John Fisher was executed. Of course, he is no longer a bishop. I took that honour away from him. The old chap used to be my teacher, in my childhood, but that couldn't save him. He DARED to say I could not be head of my own church.

The new Pope, Paul III, made Thomas a cardinal — a top Catholic leader. He thought I would never execute a cardinal. He wanted to send a cardinal's red hat to Fisher in prison.

I joked that Fisher would be wearing it on his neck... rather a good jest, don't you think?

Pope's Hope   My Plan

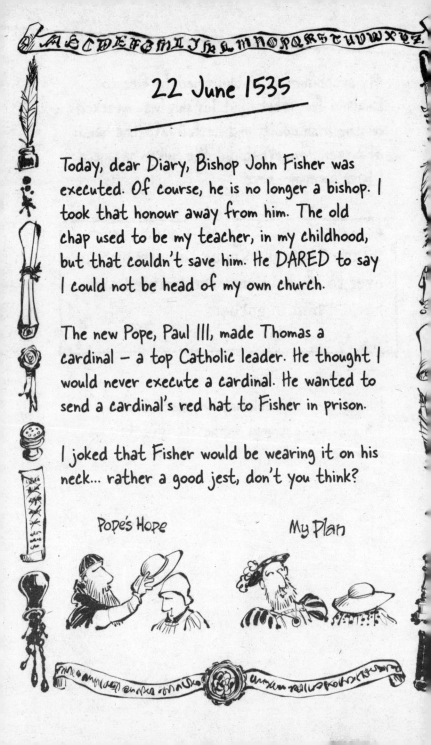

Fisher's crime was Treason. And since he is no longer a bishop, he was sentenced to a traitor's death. A traitor would be hanged, drawn and quartered. That's what happened last Saturday – 19 June 1535 – to three monks. They were:

1. half-hanged until they were half-dead
2. cut down and laid on the ground
3. cut open and their bowels drawn out then thrown on to a fire
4. before they were finally beheaded

I had kept those monks chained, forced to stand in their cells for weeks before they were executed. Cromwell made sure they were fed because we wanted them to suffer then die in public. It would not have been so much fun if they had died of hunger, would it?

But by the time Fisher came to be executed, the soft-hearted people of London were in a mood for rebellion. If old Fisher had to die, they muttered, he should be given a quick death. So, in my kindness, I had him beheaded on Tower Hill instead. NOT that I am afraid of the people of London. I just felt sorry for dear old John. Good Thomas Cromwell showed me a letter Fisher had written to him from the Tower of London...

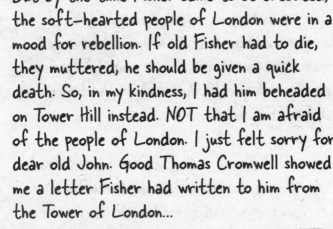

John Bishop of Rochester to Thomas Cromwell.

I beg you to be a good friend to me in my hour of need. I have no shirt or sheet or clothes except ones that be ragged and torn too shamefully. I would not mind that if they would keep my body warm. But the little food I get is poor. At my age my stomach needs just a little meat, or I fall into coughs and diseases of my body and cannot keep myself strong. His brother Please ask the King to take me from this cold and painful imprisonment. Please tell his majesty I wish him a merry Christmas.

At the Tower, 22 Dec 1534.

I have been told Fisher was taken to his execution on a donkey. The block was not ready, so he had to sit and shiver as he waited. They say that when Fisher walked to the block he staggered because he was so weak from hunger.

After the beheading, his body was stripped and left beside the block till nightfall then thrown into an open grave. A nice touch, don't you think? All my idea. But as I am 'head of the church', anyone who argues is 'head on the block'. (Another of my excellent jests, and rather poetic, I'd say.)

I should have sent that head to Rome so the Pope could put the cardinal's hat on it himself. I didn't. I am too kind.

Fisher's head shall be put on a spike over the gateway to London Bridge. My good friend, Thomas More, will be next. Fisher will have More's head for company very soon.

Archbishop Cranmer is a much better bishop of my new Church of England. Cranmer's the wonderful chap who gave me an official divorce from Catherine of Aragon a couple of years ago.

Archbishop Cranmer

6 July 1535

Thomas More is dead. Another dear friend who refused to give up the Pope and accept me as head of the church.

I read a letter he wrote to one of my ministers...

> *You often boast to me that you have the King's ear and often have fun with him, freely. This is like having fun with tamed lions – often it is harmless, but just as often there is fear of harm. Often, he roars in rage for no known reason, and suddenly the fun becomes deadly.*

You see, dear Diary? Thomas KNEW how dangerous I can be, yet he still tried to stand against me. He even wrote to dear Thomas Cromwell when Cromwell became my favourite minister. Thomas More wrote...

> If the lion knew his own strength, then it would be hard for any man to rule him.

Well, this lion has roared, and More is dead. He should have been hanged, drawn and quartered but I was merciful as ever. I said he could be simply beheaded. I wasn't there, of course, but the executioner has reported...

When Sir Thomas More came to climb the steps to the scaffold, the steps were shaky and we all feared they would collapse. Sir Thomas said to me, I pray you, master executioner, see me safe up. As for my coming down, let me look after that for myself.

I thought that was a strange thing to say till someone told me it was Sir Thomas having a joke.

He spoke to the people and said he was a true servant to you, the King and then he prayed. I asked for his pardon, then More rose up with a smile, kissed me and forgave me. As he laid his head on the block, he moved his beard out of the way and said, 'My beard was completely innocent of any crime, and does not deserve the axe.' I'm not sure a man on the scaffold should be making so many jokes. He placed his beard so that it would not be harmed.

More asked that his daughter Margaret Clement be given his headless corpse to bury because he knew I'd be fixing his head on a pike over London Bridge for a month.

I removed his head with one clean blow. The head is on London Bridge where all traitors heads belong.

Anonymous.

I shall miss Thomas More.

10 October 1536

News just in from Antwerp. That wicked William Tyndale, who wrote the Bible in English, has been executed in Flanders. The letter from there arrived this morning and said ...

> *This morning Tyndale was strangled to death while tied at the stake, and then his dead body was burned. His final words, spoken at the stake in a loud voice, were 'Lord, open the King of England's eyes'.*

How dare the man? Strangling was too good for him. If he'd been caught in England, I'd have burned him alive.

His last words would not have been about opening my eyes. They would have been screams and begging me for mercy.

Another rat in England's nest has been destroyed. Many more will follow.

31 December 1536

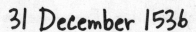

> Westminster Palace
> London

My dearest Margaret,

Greetings for the Christmas season. And let us hope 1537 is better than this year has been.

We have a lot in common — both of us have seen babies die, married in secret and lost marriage partners to divorce and death. (I'm still sorry my armies killed your husband at Flodden, but it was all his own fault.) Anyhow, this year has been seriously bad.

7 January:
My first wife Catherine died. She was living peacefully at a castle I gave to her. I liked the woman, but she could never give me the son, the heir, that I needed. All she produced

was a daughter, Mary. Even Anne could only give me a daughter, Elizabeth. There are wicked stories that say Anne sent Catherine a barrel of beer as a Christmas gift, that it was poisoned and killed my first wife. Nonsense, of course.

24 January:
I was having a joust at Greenwich Palace when my horse fell and threw me to the ground. They say I was out cold for two hours and couldn't speak.

Greenwich Palace

I wasn't knocked off and beaten. I fell. I fell. I don't lose in the jousting.

29 January:

Catherine's funeral. My wife Anne was due to have our baby son – the one I longed for. But my fall shocked her so horribly, she gave birth too early and the child died. I am doomed. Cursed not to have a son. Well, not with Anne.

Jane Seymour

10 February:

On this day I found an answer to my problem with Anne and the baby. I met Jane Seymour. A fine lady who would make a fine mother to my son, if only I were not stuck with Anne.

March:

I decided it was time to close the monasteries. They were supposed to be houses of prayer, but they are houses that just make money from their lands. The money goes to the Pope in Italy. English money from the hard-working peasants of our land. I shall close them, and all that wealth shall come to me. They are wicked men, those monks.

30 April:
I discovered that Anne had a favourite musician. A man called Mark Smeaton. I'll swear she had flirted with him and probably kissed him. This is treason. Thomas Cromwell took Smeaton away to be questioned. I hoped he was not too gentle with the man. I did see a way forward with Jane Seymour, of course.

19 May:
It was all over so quickly. Smeaton talked and Anne was sentenced to death. Instead of having her butchered on the block I sent for an expert French swordsman who took off her head with a stroke of his sword. I didn't watch.

I went off for a game of tennis. The next day, I married Jane.

7 June:
My new queen, Jane, and I went from Greenwich to York Place, at Westminster, by barge. Every lord in his own barge, and as we passed by the ships in the Thames every ship shot guns. At the Tower of London there were over four hundred guns, and all the tower walls towards the water side were set with great streamers and banners. (The very tower where Anne was rotting underground, buried in a rusting old arrow box.) She would have enjoyed the music and colour and cheering. Oh, how my people love me and my new queen.

23 July:
As you know, 17 years ago, I had a son — Henry Fitzroy. I wasn't married to his mother, but he could have been King if I had chosen him. What did the boy do on this day? He died. WHY am I so unlucky?

1 October:

You, Margaret, have faced rebels. Now, I have my own rebels to deal with. Catholics in Lincoln have risen up because they want to worship their Pope. I will not have it. But I must be careful. They have 30,000 followers and I do not have a large army. I must be cunning as a fox. Their leader, Robert Aske, is a one-eyed man. That is why I don't see eye-to-eye with him. (Just my little jest, Margaret.)

And so, Christmas has found me a miserable monarch. I have won a beautiful wife but have lost so much more this year. Why am I so very unlucky?

Your loving brother,

Henry

3 February 1537

The rebellion in Ireland is finally over. My rebel cousin, Silken Thomas, said he'd surrender if I spared his life. I told him yes — that I would NEVER execute one of my family. That was just over a year ago. I locked him in the Tower of London.

I let him live, as I promised. I let him live for a year. Today, I had him hanged, drawn and quartered. Oh, I hate having to execute my own family. But what else could I do, dear Diary?

With Silken Thomas out of the way I can now get on with my big plan. Closing down the monasteries. Monks have no place in my new Church of England. They say they are holy men, but they are not. I have read my history books and some of the reports are shocking. Look at this old letter about nuns...

My dear abbess,

I was shocked and horrified on my visit to your convent. I expected to see holy women, simply and modestly dressed. What did I find?

Nuns who crimped their hair with curling irons
Nuns wearing brightly coloured head dresses laced with ribbons down to their ankles
Nuns with sharpened fingernails like hawks

I hope these disgraceful practices will cease immediately.

And many monks were no better. The monk historian Bede told the story of Coldingham monastery in Northumbria...

The cells that were built for praying were turned into places of feasting and drinking.

A Celt called Adamnan warned that he had a dream in which he saw the monastery destroyed. The Coldingham monks behaved themselves for a while after Adamnan's warning.

Then they went back to their old ways and the monastery was destroyed by fire in 679 AD. Bede said the fire was God's punishment.

In 734, Bede himself was writing to the Bishop of York complaining...

Your Grace,

As you are aware a monk vows to lead a single life, without the company of women. I was disgusted to note that monks in one of your monasteries were not only married – they were living in the monastery with their wives and children. They are guilty of laughter, jokes, stories, feasting and drunkenness. Novice monks at Monkwearmouth monastery were having a

> *wild time hunting foxes and hares. How wicked to leave the service of Christ for a fox hunt.*

I cannot bear drunkenness. It is worse when the drunkards are monks ... monkards, you might say.

(Oh, dear Diary, I do love my jests.)

Some people are saying that when I close the monasteries, their riches and their land will all be mine. They say that I shall be rich and that is the REAL reason I am closing them. But I am a good man and I am closing these wicked places because I want to do God's work. You believe me, dear Diary, don't you?

24 October 1537

My lovely wife Jane is dead. She died today. Why am I cursed with my marriages? It's the monks. The monks, monks, monks. I shall have my revenge.

At least Jane gave me our son, Edward, two weeks ago. Now my enemies cannot kill me because, if they do, another Tudor king will take my place. Poor little motherless Edward will be a great king when I die in about 50 years.

But I won't live that long if my enemies do kill me. The Catholic traitors.

First, I have to clear away the Catholic traitors. Last year, they rebelled against my new Church of England. 30,000 northern people gathered, wanting to march on London.

These Pilgrims carried banners and wore

Pilgrimage Banner

badges that showed the bleeding wounds of Christ — but they said they weren't bloodthirsty. In fact, their leader, Robert Aske, said they were ordinary men and women who wanted to make a peaceful protest.

I was in trouble. My army chief, the Duke of Suffolk, had no men to spare to attack Aske. Only one man could save me. And he did. That man was ... Robert Aske.

Aske said he was not a rebel and he didn't want to destroy me. He wrote down a list of what his rebels did want...

THE PILGRIMAGE OF GRACE

We are not going on our Pilgrimage of Grace for earthly gains.

WE ARE DOING IT...
- for the love of Almighty God,
- for his true Catholic Church
- and for the future of that church.

WE WISH TO DO THIS BY ...
- preserving King Henry and his family
- by driving out all wicked lords
- sacking the King's evil ministers.

I am too wise to be tricked by a fool like Aske. He I told him to come and see me. I promised I wouldn't harm him. I told Aske...

Look, tell your lads, that if you all go home peacefully, I'll look at your complaints. I will also pardon you ... as long as you make no more trouble.

Aske believed me. And that gave me time to gather my forces. Some peasants in Cumberland marched on Carlisle and said they were part of the 'Pilgrimage of Grace' (though they weren't). That was just the excuse I had been waiting for.

I sent in my new army and attacked ruthlessly. Places like Sawley Monastery had been re-opened by the Pilgrims — my men took

the monks and hanged them from the steeple of the church so everyone could see what happened to rebels.

On 12 July, Aske was executed in York. He was hanged in chains from the castle walls till he starved to death. Hundreds of his supporters were hanged and a woman was even burned.

Aske has asked for it!

It is better to be feared than loved.

When I closed the small monasteries, they had their Pilgrimage of Grace. Now I shall teach them a lesson. It is time to start closing the large monasteries. Monks, monks, monks. I will be rid of them ALL.

19 May 1539

Today, dear Diary, I signed a new law to close the large monasteries. I told you that I'd have my revenge and I have.

You remember, I executed quite a few people because they read the Tyndale Bible in English. Maybe I was a bit harsh. Now we have a new Bible, and it's in English. Cromwell has sorted for me. It's written by a clever chap called Myles Coverdale. The law went out to every priest in every church...

You must provide one book of the bible in English, and set it up in some place within the church that you are in charge of. The people of your parish must be free to read it.

The peasants can't read, of course, but the priests can read it to them. It's a shame about Tyndale and people like Thomas Bilney

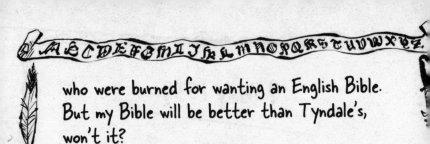

who were burned for wanting an English Bible. But my Bible will be better than Tyndale's, won't it?

I am such a kind and holy king.

Now I must turn my thoughts to more important matters. I need to find myself a new wife since dear Jane has died. I wept for Jane, of course I did. I thought I'd never get over her, but oddly I have.

There is a woman called Anne from Cleves in Flanders that Cromwell thinks may be a good match.

I told him to get on with it.

28 July 1540

Thomas Cromwell died today. On the block. I had to have him executed.

My darling Jane Seymour died three years ago after giving me my precious son, Edward. But I still need a queen to share my royal duties. It was Cromwell who was given the job of finding me someone suitable. A noble lady, obviously. And a beauty, of course.

He found me Anne Of Cleves — the sister of a duke. He showed me her picture:

Anne of Cleves

Cromwell told me she was a beauty. On New Year's Day, I finally met her. I liked her not. She was from Flanders and they are famous for their horses. I think they sent me a mare from Flanders in place of a noble lady.

How she really looks!

I had agreed with her brother that I would marry her and on 6 January, I DID marry her. I didn't like to break a promise.

But, oh dear, I just couldn't bear to have her as a wife. I like clever ladies, and poor Anne was ignorant. She was only good at needlework and card games. She DID teach me the card game of 'Mumchance', which I enjoy.

YOU NEED:

a pack of playing cards

two or more players

TO PLAY:

- the cards are shuffled and placed face down on a table
- each player in turn calls the name of a card – everyone has to name a different card
- the cards are turned over one at a time
- the player whose card is turned over first wins a point
- first to ten points is the winner

ADVANCED PLAY:

Do not shuffle the cards each time but place the turned cards to one side.
Good players will remember which cards have been turned over and will not name them.

A charming lass, and a good friend, but not a queen for such a great king as I. I had to divorce her, which I did on 9 July. And then it was time to deal with Cromwell for putting me in that mess.

He doesn't need a trial. I called him a traitor and that is enough. He was beheaded today.

And, of course, dear Diary, I now go to the other great business of today. A happy, happy day – except for Cromwell.

I am now off to marry my fifth wife, Kathryn Howard. A charming girl of 19 years old. I am only 49 – not old at all!

THIS time I have chosen her for myself, and she is a beauty.

She is the niece of my good friend, Thomas Howard, Duke of Norfolk. I know in my kind heart that our marriage will last for as long as I live. I expect that to be another 50 years. Happy, happy day today.

Except for Thomas Cromwell.

27 May 1541

Do you know, dear Diary, I sometimes think I should be an executioner at the Tower of London. I'm too busy or I WOULD do it. The fellers that are there are absolutely useless.

I have just had a report from the Constable of the Tower, Sir John Gage. A chap I can trust. He let me draw his portrait last year. A fine piece of art if I do say so myself.

Sir John Gage

It's the asses he has working for him. The jailers. Or should I call them his donkeys? I mean to say, how hard is it to cut someone's head off with an axe?

That traitor Reginald Pole has been stirring up trouble with that awful man, the Pope. But he's been stirring it up in Rome where I can't get my hands on him. He HAS to be punished. So, I've decided to execute his mother instead. That will teach him not to tangle with a Tudor.

The woman was upset, I can tell you. She said she wasn't to blame. Hah, I told her, you ARE to blame for having a son, aren't you? She had no answer to that. So, what did she do? She wrote a poem on the wall of her cell in the Tower. I have a copy here...

For traitors on the block should die.
I am no traitor, no, not I.
My faithfulness stands fast and so,
Towards the block I shall not go.
Nor make one step, as you shall see;
Christ in Thy Mercy, please save me

A pretty piece of poetry. But when she said she wouldn't take one step towards the block, I didn't know she MEANT it, did I? Look at his report.

The Tower of London

27 May 1541

Your Royal Highness,

The Countess Margaret Pole has been executed as you wished. Our executioner is in the north of England dealing with rebels. The only guard I had to do the job was a lad. I did not know he wasn't used to handling an axe.

The countess did not help him. When she was pushed down with her neck on the block, she turned her head every which way. She told the lad, 'If you want my head, you'll have to take it the best you can.'

When the blundering youth brought down the axe, she moved. He missed her neck the first time, gashing her shoulder. She managed to escape from the block and she was cut down by the executioner as she ran. He was forced to

hack her head and shoulders to pieces in the
most pitiful manner. It took another ten blows
to finish her off.

I write to beg you not to punish the
executioner. He was very upset.

Your loyal Constable

John Gage (Sir)

Butchers and donkeys. Remember,
this woman was nearly 70 years
old. If I hadn't had her
head cut off, it would
have soon dropped off.

I have enough problems of my own. My darling
wife, Kathryn Howard, is behaving very oddly.
There is something going on and I need to
send Archbishop Thomas Cranmer to find out
what she is up to.

I really don't have time to bother about old women upsetting my poor executioner, do I?

I wish Thomas Cromwell were by my side. He was the most faithful servant of them all. My ministers should never have executed him.

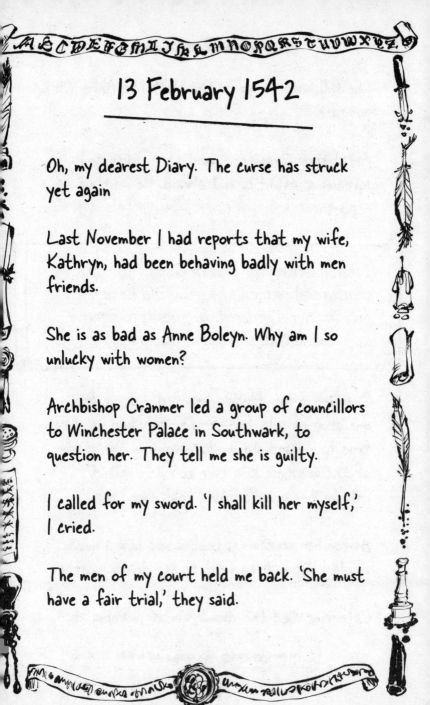

13 February 1542

Oh, my dearest Diary. The curse has struck yet again

Last November I had reports that my wife, Kathryn, had been behaving badly with men friends.

She is as bad as Anne Boleyn. Why am I so unlucky with women?

Archbishop Cranmer led a group of councillors to Winchester Palace in Southwark, to question her. They tell me she is guilty.

I called for my sword. 'I shall kill her myself,' I cried.

The men of my court held me back. 'She must have a fair trial,' they said.

She will have to go to the block like Anne. Oh, poor me.

Archbishop Cranmer found the foolish girl screaming, frantic, and afraid. He sent me a report:

> *I found her crying and in despair like no creature. Any man's heart would have felt pity for her. I ordered the guards to remove any objects that she might use to kill herself.*

Cranmer is too tender-hearted. I don't feel one drop of pity for her. She only had to stay true to me and she would have been the queen of the greatest king ever to rule England. (Maybe the greatest king that ever lived.)

As for her screaming, that is not how a queen should behave. Anne went to her death quietly.

Catherine died this dismal winter morning at

7 o'clock. They tell me she spent time last night practising how to lay her head on the block.

She must have practised well because I hear the axeman did a clean, quick job. She'll be buried next to her cousin, Anne Boleyn.

At least I have my son Edward. He's a sickly boy but he'll grow stronger and be a fine king when I die. I don't feel too well these days. I may not last 30 years.

I have two daughters too. Mary, the daughter of Catherine of Aragon, has a lady-in-waiting called Catherine Parr. This woman helps with the teaching of my children Edward and Elizabeth too.

Catherine Parr

She is not young and lively like Anne Boleyn or Kathryn Howard. But they betrayed me. She is 30 years old and has been married twice. Her mother was a friend of my first wife, Catherine of Aragon. In fact, her mother named Catherine after my first wife. I knew her when she was a child. I feel as safe with her as I would with my own mother.

Maybe Catherine Parr is the sort of woman I need. Calm and caring and clever — she has written books. It's said she is in love with my third wife's brother — Thomas Seymour. She would have to leave him, of course.

I have sent her gifts of Spanish gowns.

I am a great king and I need a great woman to be my wife.

She will not refuse me.

30 September 1544

What will the History books say about me, dear Diary? A great king who suffered a plague of wives and a plague of enemies.

The Scots are trouble. Two years ago, James V led an army into England. How dare he? Look what happened to his father at Flodden in 1513 — that seems like a lifetime ago.

We defeated his army at the battle of Solway Moss. My clever commander drove the Scots into a swamp, and they were drowned or killed or captured. We took three thousand horses, thirty banners and twenty guns. I wish I could have seen it.

The shock of the defeat killed James and left his daughter, Mary, as Queen of Scots — my niece. Of course, she was just a week old at the time. I planned to marry her off to my son Edward.

127

Then we'd have peace at last with the neighbours in the North.

But the evils Scots made a deal with my old enemy, the French. That meant I had an excuse to invade France for the third time and really show the history books what a great warrior I am. I am sick and my leg aches and my armour is tight. But I sailed across the Channel and laid siege to Boulogne. My friend, Emperor Charles V, would attack from the east while my army marched in from the west.

My fleet drew near Calais harbour on 14 July, and my ship's gunners fired round after round to announce my arrival. They were answered by cannons on the walls of the town. The thunder of guns could be heard at Dover, 25 miles away. Magnificent.

I landed, dressed in gold cloth with a red cross over my new armour and wearing a hat with crimson satin band. I could have stayed in

Calais but after two weeks, the sweating sickness broke out, so I marched on to the mighty fortress of Boulogne.

I captured Boulogne, dear Diary. I blew up its castle. I marched my brave army in. What a glorious day it was when, two weeks ago, I rode in triumph through Boulogne.

And what went wrong? Emperor Charles V went wrong. He betrayed me. Why does everyone betray me? He made peace with the French and I was trapped. I had to flee retreat back home. But you should have seen me in my finest hour, riding through Boulogne. I was a hero.

What a MARE!

The French were allowed to leave the city if they didn't want to live under English rule. I sent troops to guard them. I have heard that my troops stripped the French of their clothes to sell them and left the common people to starve and shiver in the rain.

If that is true then it is wicked, but it is what the French would do to English prisoners. I would rather slaughter fighting men with my sword. You would not find me attacking unarmed men, women and children. But I can't really stop my soldiers, can I? They know it is better to be feared than loved.

19 July 1545

And still the FRENCH plague me, tear at me, threaten and attack me.

Today, dear Diary, we are in Southampton. This morning I watched as a hundred French sails appeared on the horizon. An armada of invading ships bringing death to my people.

Armada than you!

Two hundred enemy ships in full sail. It was a fine sight. But I knew my navy would destroy them. They were led by the pride of the fleet – my ship, the Mary Rose.

That's TORN it!
DUCK!
DUCK? LOOKS MORE LIKE A SEAGULL!
RELOAD!
BOOM!
BANG!
BOOM!
FIRE!
BOOM!
HOLE IN ONE!
BANG!

She could not be sunk, my beautiful vessel. Not by the French. She was sunk by an accident. The ship was carrying a crew of 700. A breeze from the shore caught the mighty sails and she leaned over dangerously. Water began flooding into her lower gun ports. Cannons crashed across her sloping decks and made her lean still more.

In minutes, the Mary Rose sank, leaving only the tops of two masts above water.

Around 30 survivors swam for their lives. I could hear the terrible cries of crewmen trapped below decks as I looked on helplessly from Southsea Castle.

I've got tha SINKING feeling!

George Carew, the Admiral who was on another ship, has reported to say he is not to blame.

Your Majesty,

The sailors on your 'Mary Rose' were the best sailors and gunners in England when they were in battle. The trouble is they were too proud to do small jobs like closing gun ports. If you ask me, it was their fault.

The 'Mary Rose' had nets strung along the side so the Frenchies couldn't sail alongside and jump on the deck. It stopped the Frenchies getting on but, of course, it also stopped our brave sailors from getting off. And the men in armour had no chance. They sank faster than one of your golden crowns.

At least my ship saved over 30 of the sailors – the ones who weren't wearing armour, obviously.

But the French were driven off by me and the other ships. We saved England. So, you could say it was a happy ending.

Gawen Carew
(Sir George Carew's uncle)

And now I try to sleep with James V of Scotland on my mind. You'll remember that when we beat him at Solway Moss, he died from the horror of it all. Could that happen to me?

I am trying to remember the great victory tonight, dear Diary. But it is the screaming of the drowning sailors that I am hearing in my dreams. I shall think of their deaths. And my death.

Maybe I am getting too old. My legs ache. I feel too heavy to rise from my chair.

28 January 1547

The fever is making me weak. But I am strong. I will recover and rule another forty years.

My friends are all around me. Keeping me strong. Thomas More is praying for me and Thomas Cromwell is looking after the country while I rest in bed. My leg aches. It smells of rotting flesh. But it will heal and be strong once I am out of this bed, riding and hunting again.

And my dear, dear wives. They are all here to comfort me. Anne Boleyn has never left me in my sickness. She brings me water and wipes my sweating brow. She soothes me in my dreams and stands by my bed when I awake.

Over there, see Robert Aske rattling his chains. And old Countess Margaret Pole with her blood-soaked gown. They forgive me.

They knew I did what I had to do to save my life. It is better to be feared than loved. But when I recover, I may be kinder to my enemies.

And my father is here too. It would be his 90th birthday today. So good to see you, Father. So good to see you. You were a good king. But your son has been a great king.

And there are my monks, praying for my health. In the darkest corner of the room the old, dead monks are chanting prayers. They forgive me. Your popes were wicked. I had to set my English people free.

The monks, the queens, the executed enemies. Can't you see them? They're not ghosts. They are angels come to protect me. I have 30 more years to live and then they'll guide me to heaven where I belong. I have been a great king and a good man.

But now I am weary. Thank you, Anne. And you, young Kate. Thank you all. But now I am wearier than after any day out hunting. I need to rest. To sleep. To dream. And Anne will comfort me in my sleep, won't you Anne?

Goodnight to you all.

Monks, monks, monks.

This is where the diary of my husband Henry ended. His last words were, 'Monks, monks, monks.' The candle showed it was 2 o'clock in the morning. As the candle guttered and died so did Henry. The crown will pass to his son, Edward. Henry shall be buried next to Jane Seymour, Edward's mother.

We knew his death was close, but not even Henry's doctors had the courage to break the news to the King. It was, after all, treason to foretell the King's death. He was so sure he would live.

I have read this diary. It makes my husband look cruel and foolish. I shall hide it under his mattress. While I live, I will let his people believe he was a strong and powerful ruler.

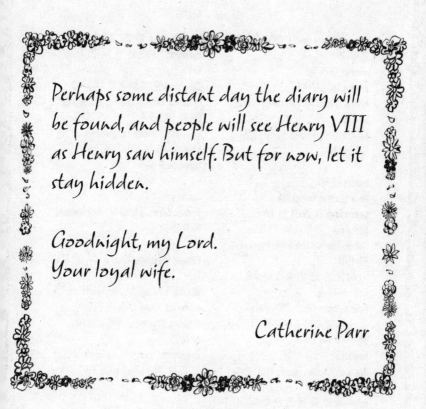

Perhaps some distant day the diary will be found, and people will see Henry VIII as Henry saw himself. But for now, let it stay hidden.

Goodnight, my Lord.
Your loyal wife.

Catherine Parr

INDEX

Tudors
rule
OK!